The Scotch Woman
Voltaire
Translation by William F. Fleming

Start Publishing PD LLC
Copyright © 2024 by Start Publishing PD LLC

All rights reserved, including the right to reproduce this book or portions thereof in any form whatsoever.

Start Publishing PD is a registered trademark of Start Publishing PD LLC
Manufactured in the United States of America

Cover art: Shutterstock/Taisiya Kozorez

Cover design: Jennifer Do

10 9 8 7 6 5 4 3 2 1

ISBN 979-8-8809-2045-7

Contents

Dramatis Personæ. 4

Act I. 5

Act II. 17

Act III. 32

Act IV. 42

Act V. 53

Represented at Paris in 1760.

Dramatis Personæ

Mr. Fabrice, master of a Coffee-house.
Miss Lindon, a Scotchwoman.
Lord Montross, a Scotchman.
Lord Murray.
Polly, maid to Miss Lindon.
Freeport, a Merchant of London.
Wasp, a Writer.
Lady Alton.
Several English Gentlemen frequenting the Coffee-house, Servants, Messengers, &c.

Voltaire dashed off this comedy in eight days, to ridicule Fréron, who had unfavorably criticised Candide. It was first published as by Hume, or Home, author of the tragedy "Douglas."

ACT I.

SCENE I.

Scene London.

The scene represents a coffee-house, with apartments on the same floor on each side communicating with it.

Wasp: [At one corner of the room reading the papers. Coffee, pen and ink, etc., on the table before him.] A plague on this vile news! here are places and pensions given to above twenty people, and nothing for me! a present of a hundred guineas to a subaltern for doing his duty! a great merit indeed! so much to the inventor of a machine to lessen the number of hands; so much to a pilot; so much settled on men of letters, but nothing for me! here's another pension, and another—but the deuce a farthing for Wasp [he throws down the paper and walks about] and yet I have done the state some service; I have written more than any one man in England; I have raised the price of paper; and yet nothing is done for me: but I will be revenged on all those whom the world calls men of merit: I have got something already by speaking ill of others; and if I can but contrive to do them a real mischief, my fortune is made. I have praised fools, and calumniated every good quality and perfection of human nature, and yet can scarce live by it: in short, to be a great man, you must not be content with slander and destruction, but endeavor to be really hurtful. [To the master of the coffee-house.] Good morrow to you, Mr. Fabrice. Well, Mr. Fabrice, everybody's affairs, I find, go well but mine; it is intolerable.

Fabrice: Indeed, indeed, Mr. Wasp, you make yourself a great many enemies.

Wasp: I believe I excite a little envy.

Fabrice: On my soul I believe not; but rather a passion of a very different kind: to be free, for I have really a friendship for you, I am extremely concerned to hear people talk of you as they do: how do you contrive to be so universally hated?

Wasp: It is because I have merit, Mr. Fabrice.

Fabrice: That may possibly be; but you are the only person who ever told me so: they say you are a very ignorant fellow: but that is nothing; they say, moreover, that you are ill-natured and malicious; that gives me concern, as it must every honest man.

Wasp: I assure you I have a good and tender heart. I do indeed now and then speak a little freely of the men; but for the women, Mr. Fabrice, I love them all, provided they are handsome. As a proof of it, I must absolutely insist on your introducing me to your amiable lodger, whom I have never yet been able to converse with.

Fabrice: Upon honor, Mr. Wasp, that young lady will never do for you; for she never praises herself, or speaks ill of anybody else.

Wasp: She speaks ill of nobody, because, I suppose, she knows nobody: are you not in love with her, Fabrice?

Fabrice: Not I indeed, sir; she has something in her air so noble, that I dare not think of it—besides, her virtue—

Wasp: [Laughing.] Ha! ha! ha! her virtue indeed!

Fabrice: Why so merry, sir? think you there is no such thing as virtue?—but I hear a coach at the door, and yonder is a livery servant with a portmanteau in his hand; some lord coming to lodge with me, perhaps.

Wasp: Be sure, my dear friend, you recommend me to him as soon as possible.

SCENE II.

Lord Montross, Fabrice, Wasp.

Montross: You, sir, I suppose, are Mr. Fabrice.

Fabrice: At your service, sir.

Montross: I shall stay here only a few days. (Protect me, heaven, unhappy as I am!) I am recommended to you, sir, as a worthy honest man.

Fabrice: So, sir, we ought all to be. You will here, sir, I believe, meet with all the conveniences of life; a tolerably good apartment, and my own table, if you choose to do me the honor to dine at it, and the amusement of coffee-house conversation.

Montross: Have you many boarders with you at present?

Fabrice: Only one young lady, sir, very handsome and extremely virtuous.

Wasp: O mighty virtuous, ha! ha!

Fabrice: Who lives quite retired.

Montross: Beauty and youth are not for me. Let me have an apartment, sir, if possible, entirely to myself. (What do I feel!) Have you any remarkable news in London?

Fabrice: This gentleman, sir, can inform you: he talks and writes more than any one man in England, and is extremely useful to foreigners.

Montross: [Walking about.] I have other business.

Fabrice: I'll step out, sir, and get things ready for you. [Exit.]

Wasp: [Aside.] This gentleman, I suppose, is just arrived in England: he must be some great man, for he seems to care for nobody. [Turning to Montross.]

Permit me, my lord, to present to your lordship my respects; my pen and self, my lord, are at your lordship's service.

Montross: I am no lord, sir: to boast of a title, if we have one, is the part of a fool; and to assume one when we have no right, that of a knave. I am what I am; but pray, sir, what may be your employment in this house?

Wasp: I don't belong to the house, sir; but I spend most of my time in the coffee-room; write news, politics, and so forth, and am always ready to do an honest gentleman service. If you have any friend you want to have praised, or any enemy to be abused; any author you want to protect or to decry; 'tis but one guinea per paragraph: if you are desirous of cultivating any acquaintance for profit or pleasure, sir, I am your man.

Montross: And have you no other business, friend?

Wasp: O sir, it is a very good one, I assure you.

Montross: And have you never been shown in public with a pretty iron collar about your neck?

Wasp: This fellow has no notion of literature.

SCENE III.

Wasp: [Sitting down to the table] several people walking about the coffee-house; Montross comes forward.

Montross: Will my misfortunes never have an end? proscribed, banished, condemned to lose my head in Scotland; in my dear native country: I have lost my honors, my wife, my son, my whole family; except one unhappy daughter, like myself a miserable wanderer, perhaps dishonored; and must I die without taking revenge on Murray's barbarous family? I am razed out of the book of life; I am no more; even my name is wrested from me by that cruel decree: I am but a poor departed ghost, that hovers round its tomb. [One of the gentlemen in the coffee-house slapping Wasp on the shoulder.] Well! you saw the new piece yesterday, it met with great applause; the author is a young fellow of merit, but has no fortune, the public ought to encourage him.

Another: Rot the new piece; public affairs are strangely carried on; stocks rise; the nation's rich, and I'm ruined, absolutely undone.

Wasp: [Writing.] The piece is good for nothing; the author's a fool, and so are all those that support him: public affairs are in a wretched condition: the nation's ruined: I shall prove it in my pamphlet.
another gentleman. Your pamphlet's nonsense: philosophy is the most dangerous thing in the world; it was that which lost us the island of Minorca.

Montross: [At a distance from them.] Lord Murray's son shall pay dearly for it. O that before I die I could avenge the father's injuries in the son's blood!

A Gentleman: I thought the comedy last night was an excellent one.

Wasp: Detestable: our taste grows worse and worse.

Another Gentleman: Not so bad as your criticisms.

Another: Philosophers sink the public funds: we must send another ambassador to Porte.

Wasp: We should always hiss a successful piece, for fear anything good should appear. [Four of them talk at once.]

First Gentleman: If there was nothing good, you would lose all the pleasure of satirizing it: now I think the fifth act has great beauties.

Second Gentleman: I can't sell any of my goods.

Third Gentleman: I am in pain for Jamaica this year: depend on't, these philosophers will make us lose it.

Wasp: The fourth and fifth acts are both contemptible.

Montross: What a riot is here.

First Gentleman: It is impossible the government can exist as it is.

Second Gentleman: If the price of Barbadoes water is not lowered, the nation's undone.

Montross: How happens it, that in every country when men meet they all talk together, though they are certain of not being heard or attended to!

Fabrice: [Enters with a napkin in his hand.] Dinner's on the table, gentlemen; but pray, let us have no disputes there, if you mean to dine with me any more. Sir, [Turning to Montross.] shall we have the honor of your company?

Montross: What, with this tribe? no, friend, let me have something in my own room. Hark'ee, sir, [Whispering to him.] Is my Lord Falbridge in London?

Fabrice: No, sir, but I believe he will be here soon.

Montross: Does he come to your house sometimes? I think I have heard so.

Fabrice: He has done me that honor.—

Montross: Very well. Good morrow to you.—How hateful is life to me! [Exit.]

Fabrice: This man seems lost in grief and thought; I should not be surprised to hear he had made away with himself; 'twould concern me, for he has the appearance of a worthy gentleman. [The gentlemen leave the coffee-house, and go to dinner; Wasp continues at the table writing: Fabrice knocks at Mrs. Lindon's door.]

SCENE IV.

Fabrice, Polly, Wasp.

Fabrice: Mrs. Polly, Mrs. Polly.

Polly: Who's there, my landlord?

Fabrice: Will you be so obliging as to favor us with your company to dinner?

Polly: I dare not, my mistress eats nothing. How indeed should we eat! we have too much grief.

Fabrice: O it will give you spirits, and make you cheerful.

Polly: I can't be cheerful: when my mistress suffers, I must suffer with her.

Fabrice: Then I'll send you up something privately. [Exit.]

Wasp: [Rising from the table.] I'll follow you, Mr. Fabrice—well, and so, my dear Polly, you will not introduce me to your mistress—still inflexible?

Polly: 'Tis a fine thing for you to pretend to make love to a woman of her condition.

Wasp: Pray what is her condition?

Polly: A respectable one, I assure you, sir. I should think a servant was good enough for you.

Wasp: That is to say, if I were to court you, you would be thankful.

Polly: Not I, indeed.

Wasp: And what, pray, is the reason why your mistress positively refuses to see me, and her waiting-maid treats me so contemptuously?

Polly: We have three reasons for it. First, you are a wit; secondly, you are very tiresome; and thirdly, you are a wicked fellow.

Wasp: And what right has your mistress, pray, who is kept here on charity, to despise me?

Polly: Upon charity? who told you so, sir? my mistress, sir, is very rich: if she is not expensive, it is because she hates pomp: she is plainly clad, out of modesty, and eats little, because temperance is prescribed to her: in short, sir, you are very impertinent.

Wasp: Don't let her give herself so many airs; we know her conduct, her birth, and her adventures.

Polly: You, sir, who told them you? what do you know?

Wasp: O, I have correspondents in every part of the world.

Polly: [Aside.] O heaven! this man will ruin us. [Turning to him.] Mr. Wasp, my dear Mr. Wasp, if you know anything, don't betray us.

Wasp: O ho! there is something then, and now I am dear Mr. Wasp: well, well, I shall say nothing, but you must—

Polly: What?

Wasp: You must love me.

Polly: Fie, fie, sir, that's impossible.

Wasp: Either love or fear me. You know there is something—

Polly: There is nothing, sir, but that my mistress is as respectable as you are hateful. We are truly easy. We fear nothing, and only laugh at you.

Wasp: They are very easy: from that I conclude they are almost starved: they fear nothing, that is to say, they are afraid of being discovered—I shall get to the bottom of it by and by, or—I shall not. I'll be revenged on them for their insolence. Despise me!

SCENE V.

Miss Lindon: [Coming out of her chamber dressed very plainly.]

Miss Lindon, Polly.

Miss Lindon: O my dear Polly, you have been with that vile fellow, Wasp; he always makes me uneasy; a destestable character, whose pen, words, and actions are all equally abominable: they tell me he works himself into families to bring in misery where there is none, and to increase it where it is: I had left this house because he frequents it, long since, but for the honesty and good heart of our landlord.

Polly: He absolutely insisted on seeing you, and I would not let him.

Miss Lindon: To see me! where is my Lord Murray, he has not been here these two days!

Polly: True, madam, but because he does not come, are we never to dine?

Miss Lindon: Remember, Polly, to conceal my misery from him, and from all the world: I am content to live on bread and water: poverty is not intolerable, but contempt is: I am satisfied to be in want, but I would not have it known I am so.

Polly: Alas! my dear mistress, whoever looks at me will easily perceive it: with you it is a different thing; your nobleness of soul supports you, you seem to rejoice in calamities, and only look the handsomer for it: but I grow thinner and thinner, you may see me fall away every minute; I am so altered within this last year that I scarcely know myself.

Miss Lindon: We must not part with our courage nor our hopes: I can support my own poverty, but yours indeed affects me. My dear girl, let the labor of my hands relieve you, we will have no obligations to anybody. Go and sell this embroidery which I have done lately. I think I succeed pretty well in this kind of work. You have assisted me, and in return my hands shall feed and clothe you: It is noble to owe our subsistence to nothing but our virtue.

Polly: Let me kiss, let me bathe with my tears the dear hands that have labored in my service O! I had rather die with my dear mistress in poverty, than be servant to a queen. Would I could administer some comfort to you!

Miss Lindon: Alas! Lord Murray is not come: he whom I ought to hate, the son of him who was the author of all my misfortunes: alas! the name of Murray will be forever fatal to me: if he comes, as he certainly will, let him not know my country, my condition, or my misfortunes.

Polly: Do you know, that villain, Wasp, pretends to be well acquainted with him?

Miss Lindon: How is it possible he should know anything of him, when even you are scarcely acquainted with him? Nobody writes to me, I am locked up in my chamber as closely as if I were in my grave: he only pretends to know something in order to make himself necessary: take care he does not so much as find out the place of my birth. You know, my dear Polly, I am an unfortunate woman whose father was banished in the late troubles, and whose family is ruined: my father is wandering from desert to desert in Scotland. I should have left London to join him in his misfortunes, but that I have still some hopes in Lord Falbridge; he was my father's friend: our true friends never desert us. He has returned from Spain, and is now at Windsor: I wait but to see him: but alas! Murray comes not. I have opened my heart to thee, remember the most fatal blow thou canst give to it would be the disclosure of my condition.

Polly: To whom should I disclose it; I never go from you; besides that, the world is very indifferent about the poor and unfortunate.

Miss Lindon: The world is indifferent, Polly, in this respect; but still it is always inquisitive, and loves to tear open the wounds of the wretched: besides that, the men assume a right over our sex when they are unhappy, and abuse their power. I would make even my miseries respectable: but alas! Lord Murray will not come.

SCENE VI.

Miss Lindon, Polly, Fabrice.

Fabrice: Forgive me, madam, I am not acquainted with your name or quality; but I have, I know not why, the greatest respect for you. I have left the company below to wait on you, and know your commands.

Miss Lindon: The regard which you express for me, my dear sir, deserves my most grateful acknowledgments: but what are your commands with me?

Fabrice: I came, madam, only to know yours: you had no dinner yesterday.

Miss Lindon: I was sick, sir, and could not eat.

Fabrice: You are worse than sick, madam, you are melancholy: you will pardon me, but I cannot help thinking your fortune is not equal to your person and appearance.

Miss Lindon: Why should you think so? I never complained of my fortune.

Fabrice: Notwithstanding that, madam, I am sure it is not what you could wish it were.

Miss Lindon: What say you?

Fabrice: I say, madam, that the world you seem to shun, admires and pities you. I am but a plain man, madam, but I can see all your merit as well as the finest courtier. Let me entreat you, my dear lady, to take a little refreshment: there is above stairs an elderly gentleman who would be glad to eat with you.

Miss Lindon: What, sit down to table with a stranger!

Fabrice: The gentleman, I am sure, would be agreeable to you: you seem afflicted, and so does he. The communication of your grief might, perhaps, give mutual consolation.

Miss Lindon: I cannot, will not, see anybody.

Fabrice: At least, madam, permit my wife to pay her respects to you, and keep you company: permit her—

Miss Lindon: I return you thanks, sir, but I want nothing.

Fabrice: You will pardon me, madam, but I cannot think you want nothing, when you stand in need even of common necessaries.

Miss Lindon: Who could make you believe so? indeed, sir, you are imposed upon.

Fabrice: You will forgive me, madam.

Miss Lindon: O Polly, 'tis two o'clock, and Lord Murray not come yet!

Fabrice: That lord you speak of, madam, is one of the best of men; you never received him here but before company. Why would not you permit me to furnish out a little repast for you both? he is, perhaps, a relative of yours.

Miss Lindon: My dear sir, you are mistaken.

Fabrice: [Pulling Polly by the sleeve.] Go, child, there is a good dinner for you in the next room. This woman is incomprehensible: but who is yonder lady in the coffee-room with a masculine air? I should have taken her for a man: how wildly she looks!

Polly: O my dear mistress! 'tis Lady Alton, who wanted to marry my lord—I remember I saw her once before this way: 'tis certainly she.

Miss Lindon: And my lord not come! then I am undone. Why am I still condemned to live? [She goes in.]

SCENE VII.

Lady Alton: [Walking across the stage in a violent passion, and taking Fabrice by the arm.] Follow me, sir, I must talk with you.

Fabrice: With me, madam?

Lady Alton: With you, wretch.

Fabrice: What a devil of a woman!

ACT II.

SCENE I.

Lady Alton, Fabrice.

Lady Alton: I don't believe a word you say, Mr. Coffeeman; you will absolutely drive me out of my senses.

Fabrice: Then pray, madam, get into them again.

Lady Alton: You have the impudence to affirm to me, that this fortune-hunter here is a woman of honor, though she has received visits from a nobleman. You ought to be ashamed of yourself.

Fabrice: Why so, madam? when my lord came, he never came in privately; she received him publicly, the doors of her apartment were open, and my wife present. You may despise my condition, madam, but you should respect my honesty; and as to the lady you are pleased to call a fortune-hunter, if you knew her, you would esteem her.

Lady Alton: Leave me, sir, you grow impertinent.

Fabrice: What a woman!

Lady Alton: [Goes to Miss Lindon's door, and knocks rudely.]

Open the door.

SCENE II.

Miss Lindon, Lady Alton.

Miss Lindon: Who knocks so? what do you want, madam?

Lady Alton: Answer me, madam. Does not Lord Murray come here sometimes?

Miss Lindon: What's that to you? what right have you to ask me? am I a criminal, and you my judge?

Lady Alton: I am your accuser. If my lord still visits you, if you encourage that wretch's passion, tremble: renounce him, or you are undone.

Miss Lindon: If I had a passion for him, your menaces, madam, would but increase it.

Lady Alton: I see you love him; that the perfidious villain has seduced you; he has deceived you, and you brave me: but know, there is no vengeance which I am not capable of executing.

Miss Lindon: Then, madam, know, I do love him.

Lady Alton: Before I revenge myself I will astonish you. There, know the traitor, look at these letters he wrote to me: there is his picture too which he gave me; but let me have it back, or—

Miss Lindon: [Giving her back the picture.] What have I seen? unhappy woman! madam—

Lady Alton: Well.

Miss Lindon: I no longer love him.

Lady Alton: Keep your resolution and your promise; know, he is inconstant, cruel, proud, the worst of characters.

Miss Lindon: Stop, madam; if you continue to speak ill of him, I may relapse, and love him again. You are come here on purpose to take away my wretched life: that, madam, will easily be done.—Polly, 'tis all over; come and assist me to conceal this last and worst of all my miseries.

Polly: What is the matter, my dear mistress, where is your courage?

Miss Lindon: Against misfortune, injustice, and poverty, there are arms that will defend a noble heart; but there is an arrow that always must be fatal. [They go out.]

SCENE III.

Lady Alton, Wasp.

Lady Alton: To be betrayed, abandoned for this worthless little wretch. [To Wasp.] You, news-writer, have you done what I ordered you? have you employed your engines of intelligence, and found out who this insolent creature is that makes me so completely miserable?

Wasp: I have fulfilled your ladyship's commands, and have discovered that she is a Scotchwoman, and hides herself from the world.

Lady Alton: Prodigious news indeed!

Wasp: I can find out nothing else at present.

Lady Alton: What service then have you been of?

Wasp: When we discover a little, we add a little; and one little joined to another, makes a great deal. There's a hypothesis for you.

Lady Alton: How, pedant, a hypothesis!

Wasp: Yes, I suppose she is an enemy to the government.

Lady Alton: Certainly, nothing can be worse inclined; for she has robbed me of my lover.

Wasp: You plainly see, therefore, that in troublesome times, a Scotchwoman, who conceals herself, must be an enemy to the state.

Lady Alton: I can't say I see it altogether so clearly, but I heartily wish it were so.

Wasp: I would not lay a wager about it, but I'd swear to it.

Lady Alton: And would you venture to affirm this before people of consequence?

Wasp: I have the honor of being related to many persons of the first fashion. I am intimate with the mistress of a valet de chambre to the first secretary of the prime minister: I could even talk with the lackeys of your lover, Lord Murray, and tell them that the father of this young girl has sent her up to London, as a woman ill disposed. Now observe, this might have its consequences, and your rival, for her bad intentions, might be sent to the same prison where I have so often been for my writings.

Lady Alton: Good, very good: violent passions must be served by people who have no scruples about them. Let the vessel go with a full sail, or let it go to the bottom. You are certainly right; a Scotchwoman who conceals herself at a time when all the people of her country are suspected, must certainly be an enemy to the state. You are no fool, as you have been represented to me. I thought you had been only a smatterer on paper, but I see you have genius. I have already done something for you; I will do a great deal more. You must let me know everything that passes here.

Wasp: Let me advise you, madam, to make use of everything you know, and of everything you do not know. Truth stands in need of some ornament: downright lies indeed may be vile things, but fiction is beautiful. What after all is truth? a conformity with our own ideas; what one says is always conformable to the idea one has whilst one is talking; therefore, properly speaking, there is no such thing as a lie.

Lady Alton: You seem to be an excellent logician, I fancy you studied at St. Omer's. But go, only tell me whatever you discover, I ask no more of you.

SCENE IV.

Lady Alton, Fabrice.

Lady Alton: This is certainly one of the vilest and most impudent scoundrels; dogs bite from an instinct of courage, and this fellow from an instinct of meanness. Methinks, now I am a little cool, his behavior makes me out of love with revenge. I could almost take my rival's part against him. She has in her low condition a pride that pleases me; she is decent, and I am told, sensible: but she has robbed me of my lover, and that I can never pardon. [To Fabrice, whom she sees in the coffee-room.] Honest man, your servant, you are a good kind of fellow, but you have got a sad rascal in your house.

Fabrice: I have heard, madam, from many, that he is as wicked as Miss Lindon is virtuous and amiable.

Lady Alton: Amiable! that wounds my heart.

SCENE V.

Fabrice, Mr. Freeport.

Fabrice: [Dressed plainly, with a large hat.] Heaven be praised, Mr. Freeport, I see you safe returned: how are you since your voyage to Jamaica?

Freeport: Pretty well, I thank you, Mr. Fabrice, I have been very successful, but am much fatigued. [To the waiter.] Boy, some chocolate and the papers—one finds it more difficult to amuse oneself than to get rich.

Fabrice: Will you have Wasp's papers?

Freeport: No: what should I do with such stuff? It is no concern of mine if a spider in the corner of a wall walks over his web to suck the blood of flies. Give me the Gazette! What public news have you?

Fabrice: None at present.

Freeport: So much the better; the less news the less folly. But how go your affairs, my friend? have you a good deal of business? who lodges with you now?

Fabrice: This morning an old gentleman came who won't see anybody.

Freeport: He's in the right of it: three parts of the world are good for nothing, either knaves or fools, and as for the fourth, they keep to themselves.

Fabrice: This gentleman has not so much as the curiosity to see a charming young lady who is in the same house with him.

Freeport: There he's wrong. Who is she, pray?

Fabrice: She is something more singular even than himself: she has now been with me these four months, and has never stirred out of her apartment: she calls herself Lindon, but I believe that is not her real name.

Freeport: I make no doubt but she's a woman of virtue, or she would not lodge with you.

Fabrice: O she is more than you can conceive; beautiful to the last degree, greatly distressed, and the best of women. Between you and me she is excessively poor, but of a high spirit and very proud.

Freeport: If that be the case she is more to blame even than your old gentleman.

Fabrice: By no means: her pride is an additional virtue. She denies herself common necessaries, and at the same time would let nobody know she does: works with her own hands to get money to pay me; never complains, but hides her tears: it is with the utmost difficulty I can persuade her to expend a little of her money, due for rent, on things she really wants; and am forced to make use of a thousand arts before she will suffer me to assist her. I always reckon what she has at half the price it cost me, and when she finds it out, there is always a quarrel between us, which indeed is the only quarrel we have ever had: in short, sir, she is a miracle of virtue, misfortune, and intrepidity: she frequently draws from me tears of tenderness and admiration.

Freeport: You are naturally tender; I am not. I admire none, though I esteem many: but I will see this woman; I am a little melancholy, and she may divert me.

Fabrice: O sir, she scarcely ever receives any visitors. There is a lord indeed who comes now and then to see her, but she will never speak to him unless before my wife. He has not been here for some time, and now she lives more retired than ever.

Freeport: I love retirement too, and hate a crowd as much as she can: I must see her, where is her apartment?

Fabrice: Yonder: even with the coffee-room.

Freeport: I'll go in.

Fabrice: You must not.

Freeport: I say I must: why not go into her chamber? bring in my chocolate and the papers. [Pulls out his watch.] I have not much time to lose, for I am engaged at two.

SCENE VI.

Freeport, Fabrice.

Miss Lindon: [frightened, Polly following her.] My God! who is this? sir, you are extremely rude; I think you might have shown more respect to my sex than thus to intrude on my retirement.

Freeport: You will pardon me, madam, [To Fabrice] bring me the chocolate.

Fabrice: Yes, sir, with the lady's consent.

Freeport: [Seats himself near a table, reads the newspaper, and looks up to Miss Lindon and Polly, takes off his hat, and puts it on again.

Polly: This gentleman seems pretty familiar.

Freeport: Why won't you sit down, madam? you see I do.

Miss Lindon: Which I think, sir, you ought not to do. I am astonished, sir: I never receive visits from strangers.

Freeport: A stranger, madam! I am very well known; my name's Freeport, a merchant, and rich: inquire of me on 'Change.

Miss Lindon: Sir, I know nobody in this country, I should be obliged to you if you would not intrude on a person to whom you are an utter stranger, and to whom as a woman you should have shown more respect.

Freeport: I don't mean to incommode you, madam: be at your ease, as I am at mine; you see I am reading the news, take up your tapestry, or drink chocolate with me, or without me, just as you please.

Polly: This is an original!

Miss Lindon: Good heaven! what a visit! and my lord not come. This whimsical fellow distracts me, and I don't know how to get rid of him. How could Fabrice let him in! I must sit down. [She sits down, and works, chocolate is brought in; Freeport takes a dish without offering her any; he sips, and talks by turns.

Freeport: Hark'ee, madam, I hate compliments, I have heard one of the best of characters of you: you are poor and virtuous, but they tell me you are proud; that's a fault.

Polly: And pray, sir, who told you all this?

Freeport: The master of this house, who is a very honest man, and therefore I believe him.

Miss Lindon: O sir, 'tis all a fable; he has deceived you; not indeed with regard to pride, which always accompanies true modesty: nor as to virtue, which is my first duty; but with regard to that poverty of which he suspects me. Those who want nothing can never be poor.

Freeport: You don't stick to truth, which is even a worse fault than being proud: I know better, I know you are in want of everything, and sometimes deny yourself so much as a dinner.

Polly: That's by order of the doctor.

Freeport: Hold your tongue, hussy, do you pretend to give yourself airs too?

Polly: What an original!

Freeport: In a word, whether you are proud or not, is nothing to me. I have made a voyage to Jamaica that has brought me in five thousand pounds: now, you must know, it is a law with me, and ought to be a law with every good Christian, always to give away a tenth part of what I get: it is a debt which I owe to the unfortunate. You are unhappy, though you won't acknowledge it. There's five hundred pounds for you: now, remember, you're paid: let me have no curtseys, no thanks, keep the money and the secret. [Throws down a large purse on the table.]

Polly: In faith this is more original still.

Miss Lindon: [Rising.] I never was so astonished in my life—alas! how everything conspires to humble me! what generosity! and yet what an affront!

Freeport: [Reading the news and drinking his chocolate.] This impertinent writer! a ridiculous fellow to talk such nonsense with an air of consequence—"The king is arrived: he makes a most noble figure, being extremely tall." The blockhead! what signifies it whether he is tall or short? could not he have told us the plain fact?

Miss Lindon: [Coming up to Freeport.] Sir—

Freeport: Well, madam—

Miss Lindon: What you have done, sir, surprises me still more than what you said: but I cannot possibly accept the money, as it may not, perhaps, ever be in my power to repay it.

Freeport: Who talks of repaying it?

Miss Lindon: I thank you, sir, for your goodness, from the bottom of my heart: you have my sincere acknowledgments, my admiration; I can no more.

Polly: You are more extraordinary than the gentleman himself. Surely, madam, in the condition you are in, deserted by all the world, you must have lost your senses to refuse an unexpected succor, thus offered you by one of the most generous, though whimsical and absurd men I ever met with.

Freeport: What do you mean by that, madam! whimsical and absurd!

Polly: If you won't accept of it for your own sake, take it for mine. I have served you in your ill-fortune, and have some right to partake of the good: in short, sir, this is no time to dissemble, we are in the utmost distress; and if it had not been for our kind landlord, must have perished with cold and hunger. My mistress concealed her condition from all those who might have been of service to us: you became acquainted with it in spite of her: in spite of herself, therefore, oblige her to accept of that which heaven hath sent her by your generous hand.

Miss Lindon: Dear Polly, you will ruin my honor.

Polly: You, my dear mistress, would ruin yourself by your folly.

Miss Lindon: If you love me, consider my reputation. I shall die with shame.

Freeport: [Reading.] What are these women prating about?

Polly: And if you love me, madam, don't oblige me to perish with hunger.

Miss Lindon: O Polly, what think you my lord would say, if still he loves me? could he believe me capable of such meanness? I always pretended to him that I wanted nothing; and shall I receive a present from another, from a stranger?

Polly: Your pretence was wrong, and your refusal still more so: as to my lord, he'll say nothing about it, for he has deserted you.

Miss Lindon: My dear Polly, by our sorrows I entreat you, do not let us disgrace ourselves: contrive in some way to excuse me to this strange man, who means well, though he is so rude and unpolished: tell him, when an unmarried woman accepts such presents, the world will always suspect she does it at the expense of her virtue.

Freeport: [Reading.] What does she say?

Polly: [Coming close to him.] O sir, something mighty ridiculous; she talks of the suspicions of the world, and that an unmarried woman—

Freeport: Is she unmarried then?

Polly: Yes, sir, and I too

Freeport: So much the better. So she says that an unmarried woman—

Polly: Cannot take a present from a man—

Freeport: She does not know what she says. Why am I to be suspected of a dishonest purpose, because I do an honest action?

Polly: Do you hear him, madam?

Miss Lindon: I hear, and I admire him, but am still resolved not to accept it: they would say I loved him; that villain. Wasp, would certainly report it, and I should be undone.

Polly: [To Freeport.] She is afraid, sir, you are in love with her.

Freeport: In love with her! how can that be, when I know nothing of her? indeed, madam, you may make yourself easy on that head; and if perchance some years hence I should fall in love with you, and you with me, well and good; as you determine, I shall determine also; and if you think no more of it, I shall think no more of it; if you tell me I am disagreeable to you, you will soon be so to me; if you desire not to see me, you shall never see me again; and if you desire me to return, I will. [Pulls out his watch.] So fare you well. I have a little business at present. Madam, your, servant.

Miss Lindon: Your servant, sir, you have my esteem and my gratitude; but take your money with you, and once more spare my blushes.

Freeport: The woman's a fool.

Miss Lindon: Mr. Fabrice, Mr. Fabrice, for heaven's sake come and assist me.

Fabrice: [Coming in a violent hurry.] What's the matter, madam?

Miss Lindon: [Giving him the purse.] Here, take this purse: the gentleman left it by mistake, give it him again, I charge you; assure him of my esteem, and remember I want no assistance from any one.

Fabrice: [Taking the purse.] O Mr. Freeport, I know you by this generous action; but be assured this lady means to deceive you: she is really in want of this.

Miss Lindon: 'Tis false: and is it you, Mr. Fabrice, who would betray me?

Fabrice: I will obey you, madam. [Aside to Freeport.] I will keep this money; it may be of service to her without her knowing it. My heart bleeds to see such virtue joined to such misfortunes.

Freeport: I feel for her too, but she is too haughty: tell her it is not right to be proud. Adieu.

SCENE VII.

Polly: Polly: Well, madam, you have made a fine piece of work of it; heaven graciously offered you assistance, and you resolve to perish in indigence; I too must fall a sacrifice to your virtue, a virtue which is not without its alloy of vanity: that vanity, madam, will destroy us both.

Miss Lindon: Death is all I have to wish for: Lord Murray no longer loves me; he has left me these three days; he has loved my proud and cruel rival; perhaps, he loves her still. I was to blame to think of him, but 'tis a crime I shall not long be guilty of. [She sits down to write.]

Polly: She seems in despair, alas! she has but too much reason to be so; her condition is far worse than mine: a servant has always some resource, but a woman like her can have none.

Miss Lindon: [Folding up her letter.] 'Tis no great sacrifice. There, Polly, when I am no more, carry that letter to him—

Polly: What says my dear mistress?

Miss Lindon: To him who is the cause of my death. I have recommended you to him, perhaps he may comply with my last request: go, Polly, [embracing her] and be assured, that amongst all my misfortunes, that of not being able to recompense you as you deserve, is not the least which this wretched heart has experienced.

Polly: O my dear mistress, I cannot refrain from tears, you harrow up my soul: what is your dreadful purpose? what means this letter? God forbid I should ever deliver it! [she tears the letter.] Alas! madam, why would not you open your heart to Lord Murray? perhaps your cold reserve has disgusted him.

Miss Lindon: Perhaps so, indeed: my eyes are open now, I must have offended him: but how could I disclose my condition to the son of him who ruined my father and family?

Polly: How, madam! was it my lord's father who—

Miss Lindon: Yes, it was he who persecuted my father, had him condemned to death, deprived us of our nobility, and took away everything from us: left as I am without father, mother, or fortune, I have nothing but my reputation and my fatal love. I ought to detest the son of Murray: misfortune, that still pursues me, brought me acquainted with him. I have loved him, and I ought to suffer for it.

Polly: O madam, you grow pale, your eyes are dim.

Miss Lindon: May grief perform that office for me, which sword or poison—

Polly: Help here, Mr. Fabrice, help: my mistress faints.

Fabrice: Help, help here! where are ye all, my wife, my servants, come down: tell the gentlemen above—help here— [Fabrice's wife, her maids, and Polly, carry off Miss Lindon into her chamber.]

Miss Lindon: [As she is going out.] Why will ye bring me back to life again? let me die in peace.

SCENE VIII.

Montross, Fabrice.

Montross: What's the matter, landlord?

Fabrice: That beautiful young lady, sir, I told you of, fainted away just now: but it will be over soon.

Montross: O the mere effect of vapors in young girls; they are not dangerous: what service could I be of? why call me down for this? I thought the house must have been on fire.

Fabrice: I had rather it were, than this sweet creature should be hurt. If Scotland has many such beauties as her, it must be a charming country.

Montross: Is she Scotch then?

Fabrice: So it seems; though I knew it but to-day: our news-writer tells me so, and he knows everything.

Montross: And what's her name?

Fabrice: She calls herself Lindon.

Montross: That's a name I'm not acquainted with. [He walks about.] The bare mention of my country rives my heart. Was ever man treated with such cruelty and injustice as I have been? Barbarous Murray, thou art dead; but thy son survives: I will have justice or revenge. O my dearest wife, my children, my daughter! I have lost all. This sword had long since ended all my cares, did not the hopes of sweet revenge force me still to bear the detestable load of life.

Fabrice: [Returning.] Thank God! all is well again.

Montross: What sudden change has happened then?

Fabrice: O, sir, she has recovered her senses, and is pretty well; looks still pale, but always beautiful.

Montross: O it's nothing. I must go out—I must run the hazard—I will. [Exit.]

Fabrice: This man does not trouble himself much about young ladies that faint; but if he had seen Miss Lindon, he would not be so indifferent.

ACT III.

SCENE I.

Lady Alton, Andrew.

Lady Alton: Yes: since I can't see the villain at home, I'll see him here: he'll certainly come. This news-writer told me truth, and was in the right of it: a Scotchwoman concealed in these dangerous times! she must be in a conspiracy against the state; she shall be seized; the order is given; at least I am too sure she conspires against me: but here comes Andrew, my lord's servant; I will know the whole of my misfortune. Andrew, you have got a letter from my lord, have not you?

Andrew: Yes, madam.

Lady Alton: For me.

Andrew: No, madam.

Lady Alton: How? have not you brought me several from him?

Andrew: Yes, madam: but this is not for you; 'tis for a certain person whom he is most desperately in love with.

Lady Alton: Well, and was not he most desperately in love with me when he used to write to me?

Andrew: O no, madam, he loved you calmly and coldly; 'tis quite another thing here; he neither sleeps nor eats, runs about day and night, and does nothing but talk of his dear Lindon. O there's a great deal of difference, I assure you.

Lady Alton: Perfidious wretch! but no matter: I tell you that letter is for me: 'tis without a superscription, is not it?

Andrew: Yes, madam.

Lady Alton: Were not all the letters you brought me without a superscription too?

Andrew: Yes, madam; but this I know is for Miss Lindon.

Lady Alton: I tell you 'tis for me, and to prove it to you, here are ten guineas for you.

Andrew: Indeed, madam, I begin to think the letter was for you; I was certainly mistaken: but if after all it is not, I hope you will not betray me; you may say you found it at Miss Lindon's.

Lady Alton: O leave that to me.

Andrew: After all, where is the harm in giving a love letter designed for one woman to another? they are all alike; and if Miss Lindon does not receive this letter, she may have twenty others. I have executed my commission, and made a pretty good hand of it too.

Lady Alton: [Opens the letter, and reads.] Now for it—"My dear, amiable, and truly virtuous Miss Lindon"—that's more than ever he said to me—" 'tis now two days, an age to me, since I had the happiness of seeing you: but I have denied myself that pleasure with the hopes of serving you. I know what you are, and what I owe you. I will change the face of your affairs, or perish in the attempt. My friends are zealous for you. Depend on me as on the most faithful of lovers, and one who will endeavor to prove himself worthy of your affection."

This is an absolute conspiracy; there can be no doubt of it: she is a Scotchwoman, and her family ill disposed to the government. Murray's father commanded in Scotland: his friends, he says, are zealous; he runs about day and night: 'tis certainly a conspiracy. Thank God, I am as zealous as he, and if she does not accept my offers, she shall be seized in an hour's time, before her vile lover comes to her assistance.

SCENE II.

Lady Alton, Miss Lindon, Polly.

Lady Alton: [To Polly, who is passing from her mistress's apartment towards the coffee-room.] You, madam, go immediately and tell your mistress I must speak with her; she need not be afraid; I shall say nothing to her but what will be agreeable, and concerns her happiness: let her come immediately, immediately, do you hear? she need not be afraid, I say.

Polly: O madam, we are afraid of nothing; but your looks make me tremble.

Lady Alton: I'll see if I can't persuade this virtuous lady to do as I would have her: I'll make my proposals, however.

Miss Lindon: [Comes in trembling, supported by Polly.] What are your commands with me, madam? are you come again only to insult me in my distress?

Lady Alton: No: I come to make you happy. I know you are worth nothing; I am rich; I now make you an offer of one of my seats on the borders of Scotland, with all the lands belonging to it; go and live there, you and your family, if you have any; but you must immediately quit my lord forever, nor must he know of your retreat as long as you live.

Miss Lindon: Alas! madam, he has abandoned me: be not jealous of a poor unfortunate: in vain you offer me a retreat; I shall soon find one without you, an eternal one, in a place where I need not blush at my obligations to you.

Lady Alton: Rash woman, is this an answer for me?

Miss Lindon: Rashness, madam, would ill suit with my condition; firmness and intrepidity will much better become it: my birth, madam, is as good as yours; my heart, perhaps, much better; and as to my fortune, it shall not depend on any one, much less on my rival. [Goes out.]

Lady Alton: [Alone.] It shall depend on me. I am sorry she reduces me to this extremity, and am ashamed to make use of this rascal, Wasp; but she obliges me to it. Faithless lover! unhappy passion! O! I am choked with rage.

SCENE III.

Fabrice, Lady Alton, Freeport, Montross [in the coffee-room, with Fabrice's wife, and servants putting things in order.]

Lady Alton: [To Fabrice.] Mr. Fabrice, you see me here often; but 'tis your own fault.

Fabrice: On the contrary, madam, we could wish—

Lady Alton: I am more concerned than you can be; but you shall see me again, I assure you. [She goes out.]

Fabrice: So much the worse. What would she be at now? What a difference there is betwixt her and the beautiful patient Miss Lindon!

Freeport: True; she is, as you say, beautiful and virtuous.

Fabrice: I am sorry this gentleman never saw her; I am sure he would be greatly affected with her behavior.

Montross: [Aside.] Wretch that I am! I have other things to think of.

Freeport: I am always either on 'Change or at Jamaica; but one can't help liking now and then to see a fine woman: she is really a fine creature, a sweet behavior, a charming countenance, and has something noble in her air and demeanor.—I must see her again one day or other. 'Tis pity she's so proud.

Montross: My landlord here informs me you behaved to her in a most generous manner.

Freeport: Who I? no. Would not you, or any man in my place, have done the same?

Montross: If I had been rich, and she had merit, I believe I might.

Freeport: What is there in it then to be wondered at? [He takes up the papers.] Well, what news have we to-day? How's this? Lord Falbridge dead!

Montross: Falbridge dead! the only friend I had on earth, or from whom I could expect relief? O fortune, fortune, wilt thou ever persecute me?

Freeport: Was he your friend? I am sorry for you.—"Edinburgh, April 14. Great search is being made after Lord Montross, condemned to lose his head about eleven years ago."

Montross: Just heaven! what do I hear? What's that, sir, Lord Montross condemned—

Freeport: Yes, sir, Lord Montross; there, sir, read it yourself.

Montross: [Looking on the paper.] 'Tis so indeed. [Aside.] I must get away as fast as I can; this place is too public: sure, earth and hell conspired together never heaped so many misfortunes on one man. [To his servant.] John, let my horses be saddled, perhaps I may be going towards evening—how bad news flies!

Freeport: Bad news, why so? what signifies it whether Lord Montross is beheaded or not? everything passes away—to-day a head is cut off, to-morrow we have it in the newspapers, and next day we talk no more of it. If this Miss Lindon was not so proud, I would go and ask her how she did; she is very handsome, and a very worthy creature.

SCENE IV.

To them a King's Messenger.

Messenger: Is your name Fabrice, sir?

Fabrice: Yes, sir, your commands with me?

Messenger: You keep a coffee-house, and let lodgings?

Fabrice: I do, sir.

Messenger: You have a young Scotch lady in your house, named Lindon?

Fabrice: I have, sir, and esteem it a great happiness.

Freeport: A most beautiful and virtuous lady; everybody tells me so.

Messenger: I come to seize her by order of the government; there's my warrant.

Fabrice: Amazing! I shudder at the thought.

Montross: A young Scotchwoman seized on the very day of my arrival! O my unhappy family, my country, what will become of my unfortunate daughter! she is, perhaps, the victim of my misfortunes, languishing in poverty and a prison: why was she ever born?

Freeport: I never heard of young girls being seized by order of the government: I am afraid, Mr. Messenger, you are a rascal.

Fabrice: If she is a fortune-hunter, as Wasp said, it will ruin my house; I am undone: this court lady had some reasons I see plainly—and yet she must be good and virtuous.

Messenger: Let's have none of your reasons, sir, to prison, or give bail, that's the rule.

Fabrice: I'll give you bail, myself, my house, my goods, my person.

Messenger: Your person's nothing; the house, perhaps, not your own—your goods, where are they? I must have money.

Fabrice: Good Mr. Freeport, shall I give him the five hundred pounds which she so nobly refused, and which are still in my possession?

Freeport: Ay, ay, I'll give five hundred, a thousand, two thousand; I'll be answerable for it, my name's Freeport. I believe the girl's strictly virtuous; but she should not be so proud.

Messenger: Come, sir, give us your bond.

Freeport: With all my heart.

Fabrice: 'Tis not every one employs their money thus.

Freeport: To spend it in doing good is putting it out to the best interest. [Freeport and the Messenger retire to the corner of the coffee-room to count out the money.]

SCENE V.

Montross, Fabrice.

Fabrice: You are astonished, sir, at Mr. Freeport; but 'tis his constant practice: happy are those whom he takes a fancy to! he is no complimenter, but does a man a service in less time than others spend in making protestations about it.

Montross: [Aside.] There are still in the world some noble souls—what will become of me?

Fabrice: We must take care not to let the poor young lady know anything of the danger she has been in.

Montross: I must be gone this night.

Fabrice: One should never tell people of their danger till it is past.

Montross: The only friend I had in London is dead: what should I do here?

Fabrice: We should make her faint away a second time.

SCENE VI.

Montross: A young Scotchwoman is seized, a person who lives retired, and is suspected by the government. I don't know why, but this adventure throws me into deep reflections. Everything conspires to awaken the memory of my sorrows, my afflictions, my misfortunes, and my resentment.

SCENE VII.

Montross: [Seeing Polly crossing the stage.] One word with you, madam, are you that pretty amiable young lady, born in Scotland, who—

Polly: Yes, sir—I, I am tolerably young, and a Scotchwoman; and as to pretty they say I am not amiss.

Montross: Have you any news from your own country?

Polly: No, sir, I have left it a long time.

Montross: And what are your relations, pray?

Polly: My father was an excellent baker, as I have heard, and my mother waiting-maid to a woman of quality.

Montross: O, now I understand you. You, I suppose, are servant to that young lady I have heard so much of. I was mistaken.

Polly: O sir, you do me too much honor.

Montross: You know who your mistress is, I suppose?

Polly: Yes, sir, the sweetest and most amiable of her sex, and one too who has the most fortitude in affliction.

Montross: She is in distress then?

Polly: Yes, sir, and so am I: but I had rather serve her in affliction than be ever so happy.

Montross: But don't you know her family?

Polly: My mistress, sir, desires to remain unknown: she has no family: sir, why do you ask me these questions?

Montross: To remain unknown! say you? O heaven, if I could at last—but 'tis a vain imagination. Tell me, pray, how old is your mistress?

Polly: One may safely tell her age. She is just eighteen.

Montross: Eighteen! the very age of my dear Montross, my lovely infant, the only remaining hope of my unhappy family—eighteen sayest thou?

Polly: Yes, sir, and I am but two and twenty, there's no great difference between us. I see no reason why you should make so many reflections on her age.

Montross: Eighteen, and born in my country, desires to remain unknown! I cannot contain myself—by your permission I must see and talk to her immediately.

Polly: Telling him of a girl of eighteen has turned this old gentleman's brain.—You can't possibly see her at present, sir, she's in the greatest distress.

Montross: For that very reason I must see her.

Polly: O, sir, fresh griefs and calamities have torn her heart, and deprived her of her senses. She is not one of those I assure you, sire, who faint away for nothing; she is but just now come to herself, and the little rest she now enjoys is mixed with grief and bitterness. Have pity, sir, on her condition.

Montross: All you say but increases my desire. I am her countryman, and partake of her afflictions, perhaps I may be able to lessen them; permit me, I beg you, before I leave this place, to have an interview with her.

Polly: You affect me deeply, sir; stay here a few minutes. It is impossible a young lady, who has just fainted away, should be able to receive visits immediately. I'll go to her, and come back to you soon.

SCENE VIII.

Montross, Fabrice.

Fabrice: [Pulling him by the sleeve.] Sir, is there nobody near us?

Montross: With what impatience shall I wait for her return!

Fabrice: Can nobody hear us?

Montross: I can never support this anxiety.

Fabrice: They are in search of you, sir,—

Montross: Who, where, what?

Fabrice: I say, sir, they are in search of you; I cannot help interesting myself in the safety of those who lodge in my house. I don't know who you are, sir, but I have been asked a thousand questions about you. They have surrounded the house, passing, and repassing, getting all the information they can. In short I shall not be surprised if in a little time they should pay you the same compliment as they did the young lady, who, it seems, is of the same country.

Montross: I must speak with her before I go.

Fabrice: Take my advice, sir, and get away as fast as you can; our friend, Freeport, perhaps might not be in the humor to do as much for you as for a girl of eighteen.

Montross: Pardon me, but I know not where I am; I scarce heard you—what must I do, or where can I go? my dear sir, I cannot go without seeing her: let me talk to you a little in private: I must beg you some how or other to let me have an opportunity of seeing this young lady.

Fabrice: I told you before, you would want to see her. I assure you nothing can be more beautiful, more virtuous, or more agreeable.

ACT IV.

SCENE I.

Fabrice, Wasp: [At a table in the coffee-room.]

Freeport: [Smoking a pipe.]

Fabrice: I must be so free as to tell you, Mr. Wasp, if I may believe all that is said of you, you would do me a favor by never coming to my house again.

Freeport: All that is said is generally false: what fly has stung you, Mr. Fabrice?

Fabrice: You come, and write your papers here, Mr. Wasp; and my coffee-house will be looked on as a poison shop.

Freeport: [To Fabrice.] This fellow seems to deserve what you say.

Fabrice: [To Wasp.] They say you speak ill of all mankind.

Freeport: Of all mankind! that's too much indeed.

Fabrice: They begin even to say you are an informer, and a scoundrel, but I am loth to believe them.

Freeport: [To Wasp.] Do you hear, sir? this is past raillery.

Wasp: I am an illustrious writer, sir, a man of taste.

Fabrice: Taste or no taste, sir, I say you have done me an injury.

Wasp: So far from it, sir, that I have helped off your coffee, made it fashionable to come to your house, 'tis my reputation that has brought you custom.

Fabrice: A fine reputation indeed! that of a spy, a bad author, and a worse man!

Wasp: Stop, Mr. Fabrice, if you please. You may attack my morals, but my works—I will never suffer that.

Fabrice: Your writings, sir, are not worth my consideration; but you are suspected of a design against the amiable Miss Lindon.

Freeport: If I thought so, I would drown the dog with my own hands.

Fabrice: 'Tis said, you accused her of being Scotch, and the honest gentleman too who lives above stairs.

Wasp: Well, and suppose I had, what harm is there in being of any particular country?

Fabrice: 'Tis moreover reported that you have had several conferences with the agents of a certain choleric lady who comes here, and with the servants of a noble lord, who used to frequent this house: that you tell tales, and blow up quarrels.

Freeport: [To Wasp.] Are you really such a rogue? then shall I detest you.

Fabrice: O thank God! here comes my lord, if I am not mistaken.

Freeport: A lord, is it? then your humble servant, I hate a lord, as much as I do a bad writer.

Fabrice: He's not like other lords, I assure you.

Freeport: Like other lords or not, 'tis no matter. I never love to be disturbed, so fare you well. I don't know how it is, my friend, but I am always thinking of this young Scotchwoman—I'll come back presently—immediately. I want to talk seriously to her—your servant. This Scotchwoman is handsome, and a good creature.—Adieu—[returning] tell her, I intend to serve her greatly.

SCENE II.

Lord Murray: [Pensive and in great agitation.]

Wasp: [Bowing to him, of which he takes no notice.]

Fabrice: [At a distance from him.]

Lord Murray: [To Fabrice.]

I'm glad to see you, friend: how is that charming girl you have the pleasure to boast of as your lodger here?

Fabrice: She has been very ill, sir, since she saw you: but I'm sure she will be better now.

Lord Murray: Great God, thou protector of innocence, I implore thee for her; O deign to make me an instrument in doing justice to virtue, and sheltering the unfortunate from oppression! Thanks to thy goodness, and my own endeavors, I have hopes of success. Hark'ee, friend, I would talk a little with that man. [Pointing to Wasp.]

Wasp: [To Fabrice.] You see, sir, you were mistaken, and I have some credit still at court.

Fabrice: [Going out.] That's not quite so clear.

Lord Murray: [To Wasp.] Well, my friend—

Wasp: [Bowing.] Permit me, my lord, to dedicate a volume to your lordship—

Lord Murray: No, sir, we are not talking about dedications: you are the person that informed my servants of the arrival of the old gentleman just come from Scotland; you described him, and made the same report to the minister of state.

Wasp: My lord, I only did my duty.

Lord Murray: [Giving him a purse.] You have done me a service without knowing it: but I don't consider the intention. Some folks say you meant to hurt, and have done good: there's something for your service. But if ever from this time forward you so much as pronounce the name of that gentleman, or of Miss Lindon, I'll throw you out at window,—away, be gone, sir.

Wasp: My lord, I return you thanks; everybody abuses me, and gives me money; I am certainly a cleverer fellow than I thought I was.

SCENE III.

Lord Murray: [Alone.] An old gentleman just arrived from Scotland; Miss Lindon born in the same country! alas! if it were possible to repair the cruel injuries my father did—if heaven would graciously permit—but I'll go in. [To Polly, who comes out of Miss Lindon's apartment.] Polly, were not you surprised at not seeing me for so long a time? two whole days! I should not have forgiven myself had I not been engaged in my dear Miss Lindon's service: the ministers of state were at Windsor, and I was obliged to follow them there. Heaven surely inspired thee, when thou toldst me, Polly, the secret of her birth.

Polly: I'm frightened yet, my mistress so often forbade me: were I to give her the least uneasiness I should die with grief. Alas! sir, your absence this very day threw her into a fainting fit, and I believe I should have fainted too, if I had not exerted all my strength to assist her.

Lord Murray: There, Polly, there's something for the fainting fit you had like to have fallen into. [Gives her money.]

Polly: My lord, I thank you; I am not so high spirited as my mistress, who refuses to accept of anything; and pretends to be quite at her ease, when she is absolutely starving.

Lord Murray: Good heaven! the daughter of Montross reduced to poverty! how guilty am I! but I will repair everything, her condition shall soon be changed: why would she so long conceal it from me?

Polly: 'Tis the only thing in which she deceived you, or I believe ever will.

Lord Murray: But let us go in, I long to throw myself at her feet.

Polly: O my lord, not yet; she is now with an old gentleman, a very old gentleman, who is her countryman, and they are saying such tender things.

Lord Murray: Who is this old gentleman? methinks I am already interested in his favor.

Polly: I know nothing of him.

Lord Murray: Would to God he were the person I wish him to be! and what did they say to each other?

Polly: They began to grow very serious, the gentleman seemed to wish me out of the room, and so I came away.

SCENE IV.

Lady Alton, Lord Murray, Polly:

Lady Alton: So, sir, at last I've caught you: thou base perfidious man, now sir, I am convinced of your inconstancy, and my own disgrace.

Lord Murray: True, madam, you are so. [Aside.] what an unseasonable intrusion!

Lady Alton: Perfidious monster!

Lord Murray: A monster I may appear in your eyes, and I am glad of it; but perfidious I never was; 'tis not my character: before I loved another, I frankly told you I had no longer any regard for you.

Lady Alton: After a promise of marriage, wretch, after so many protestations of love!

Lord Murray: When I made those protestations I loved you, and when I promised to marry you, I meant to do so.

Lady Alton: And why then did not you keep your word? what prevented you?

Lord Murray: Your character, your fiery temper and disposition: marriage was intended to make us happy, and I saw too plainly we were not made for each other.

Lady Alton: And so you have quitted me for a wandering lady errant, a poor fortune-hunter.

Lord Murray: No, madam, I leave you for softness and good-nature, for every grace, and every virtue.

Lady Alton: But you are not yet possessed of her: know, traitor, I will be revenged, and speedily too.

Lord Murray: I know your vindictive temper, know you have more envy than jealousy, more rage than tenderness, but you will be forced to honor and respect the woman I love.

Lady Alton: I know the object of your affection, sir, better than you do; know I who she is; I know too who that stranger is, who came hither yesterday: yes sir, I am acquainted with it all, and so are they who have more power and authority than Lord Murray: that unworthy rival, for whom I am despised, shall soon be seized and taken from you.

Lord Murray: What says she, Polly? I'm terrified at the thought.

Polly: And so am I. We are undone, sir.

Lord Murray: Stay, madam, explain yourself—hear me.

Lady Alton: I'll hear nothing, answer nothing, explain nothing: you are an inconstant, false-hearted, perfidious villain. [Exit.]

SCENE V.

Lord Murray, Polly.

Lord Murray: What does this fury mean? her jealousy is terrible: heaven grant I never may be jealous! she talks of having my dear girl seized, and pretends to know this stranger. What would she be at?

Polly: To tell you the truth, my mistress has been taken up by order of the government, and I too, I believe; and if it had not been for an honest fat man, who is goodness itself, and who gave in bail for us, we had both been in prison at this very time. They had made me swear not to tell you anything of it: but how can I conceal it from you?

Lord Murray: What do I hear? misfortune on misfortune! your mistress's very name I find is suspected. Alas! my family was born to be the destruction of hers: heaven, fortune, justice, and love would repair all, but guilt opposes me. It shall not, must not triumph; do not alarm my dear girl. I'll go myself to the ministry! Try everything, do everything to save her. I'll deny myself the happiness of seeing her till I can assure her of success. I fly, Polly, to serve her, and will return immediately. Tell her I have left only because I adore her. [Going out.]

Polly: This is a strange adventure. I see this world is nothing but a perpetual contest between the virtuous and the wicked, and we poor girls are always the sufferers.

SCENE VI.

Miss Lindon: [Nods to Polly, who goes out.]

Montross: Every word you utter pierces my soul: born in Lochaber! persecuted, oppressed, and deserted! a woman with such noble sentiments!

Miss Lindon: Those sentiments, sir, perhaps are owing to my misfortunes: had I been brought up in ease and luxury, my soul, which is fortified by adversity, had been weak and vain.

Montross: O thou art worthy of a nobler fate. You acknowledge to me you are sprung from one of the proscribed families, whose blood was shed on a scaffold in our civil wars. But still you conceal from me your name and birth.

Miss Lindon: Duty binds me to silence. My father himself was proscribed: they are even now in search of him, and were I to name perhaps I might destroy him. You inspire me, I own, with uncommon tenderness and respect, but I know you not, and I have everything to fear. You see I am myself suspected, and am a prisoner here. One word might ruin me.

Montross: One word perhaps might give me the greatest comfort: but tell me only what age you were of when you parted from your father, who was afterwards so unhappy?

Miss Lindon: I was then but five years old.

Montross: Great God, have mercy on me! everything she says contributes to throw new light on my dark paths! O providence, do not withdraw thy goodness from me!

Miss Lindon: You weep, sir, alas! nor can I help joining my tears with yours.

Montross: [Wiping his eyes.] Go on, I conjure you: after your father had quitted his family to see it no more, how long did you remain with your mother?

Miss Lindon: I was ten years old when she died in my arms, oppressed with grief and misery, and after she had heard that my brother was killed in battle.

Montross: O, I faint; what a dreadful moment! O thou dear, unhappy wife, and thou more fortunate son, to die without seeing so much misery! do you remember this picture? [Takes a picture out of his pocket.]

Miss Lindon: What do I see? is this a dream? surely 'tis my mother's picture.

Montross: It is, it is your mother; and I am that unhappy father who is condemned to death, whose trembling arms now embrace thee.

Miss Lindon: Do I live? where am I? O, sir, behold me at your knees: this is the first happy moment of my life: O, my father! alas! how darest you venture hither? I tremble for you, even whilst I am thus happy in your sight.

Montross: My dearest child, you know the misfortunes of our family; you know that the house of Murray, still jealous of ours, plunged us into these calamities. I have lost all: one friend alone remained, who by his interest and power might have restored me, and had promised it; but on my arrival here, I find that friend is dead, that I am searched after in Scotland, and a price put on my head. 'Tis, no doubt, the son of my old enemy who still persecutes me: I will die by his hand, or be revenged on him.

Miss Lindon: And come you then with a resolution to kill Lord Murray?

Montross: Yes: I will avenge you and my family, or die. I only hazard a life already devoted to the scaffold.

Miss Lindon: O fortune, in what new horrors dost thou involve me! what must I do? O my father!

Montross: My dearest daughter! how cruel is thy fate to be born of such a wretched father!

Miss Lindon: O sir, I am much more unhappy than you think me: are you resolved on this fatal enterprise?

Montross: Ay, to death.

Miss Lindon: O, my dear father, let me conjure you by that life which you gave me, by your misfortunes, by my own, which are, perhaps, still greater, do not expose me to the dread of losing you; have pity on me, spare your own life, and preserve mine.

Montross: Your voice reaches to my inmost soul: methinks I hear in thee, thy much-loved mother; speak, what would you?

Miss Lindon: Do not expose your precious life, but quit this dangerous place, dangerous for us both: yes, I am resolved I will renounce all for my dear father's sake. I am ready to follow you, I will accompany you, sir, to some far distant island, and there these hands shall labor to support you. It is my duty, and I will perform it: 'tis done, away.

Montross: I must not then avenge you?

Miss Lindon: No, sir, that vengeance would destroy me: come, let us be gone.

Montross: Well, I submit. The father's love prevails over all: since you have the courage to accompany me, I will go: I will prepare everything for our departure from London within this hour: be ready: one more embrace, and farewell.

SCENE VII.

Miss Lindon, Polly:

Miss Lindon: 'Tis all over, Polly: I shall never see Lord Murray again.

Polly: Indeed, madam, but you will; he'll be here in a few minutes: he is but just gone from hence.

Miss Lindon: Gone from hence! and not see me; this is worse than all. O my unhappy father! why did we not go before?

Polly: If he had not been interrupted by that detestable Lady Alton.

Miss Lindon: What! did he meet her here after all to insult me! after leaving me for three days without so much as writing! to affront me so grossly. O if my life were not necessary to my dear father, this moment would I part from it.

Polly: But hear me, madam, I swear to you my lord.—

Miss Lindon: Perfidious wretch! but all men are so. O my poor father! hereafter I will think on none but thee.

Polly: On my soul, madam, you are wrong; my lord is not false or perfidious, but one of the best of men: he loves you from his soul, and has given me convincing proofs of it.

Miss Lindon: Nature should be superior to love. I know not whither I am going, or what will become of me; but certainly I can never be more miserable than I am at present.

Polly: My dear mistress, you will hear nothing; recover your spirits a little: I tell you, you are beloved.

Miss Lindon: O Polly, will you follow me?

Polly: To the end of the world, madam: but hear me; you are beloved, indeed you are.

Miss Lindon: Let me alone; talk no more to me of my lord: alas! if he did love me, I must leave him—that gentleman you saw with me—

Polly: Well—

Miss Lindon: Come in, and I'll tell you all: tears and sighs will not let me speak: follow me, and get everything ready for our departure.

ACT V.

SCENE I.

Miss Lindon, Freeport, Fabrice.

Fabrice: Polly, I find, is packing up your things; you are going to leave us: you can't imagine, madam, the concern it gives me.

Miss Lindon: My dear landlord, and you, sir, to whom I am so much indebted for your unmerited generosity, I am sorry it is not in my power to return it; but be assured I shall never, whilst I have life, forget you.

Freeport: What is all this, what is all this? if you like us, why do you leave us? you aren't afraid of anything are you? a girl, like you, can have nothing to fear.

Fabrice: Mr. Freeport, the old gentleman, who it seems is her countryman, is going too. The lady wept, and he wept, at parting; and I am ready to weep too.

Freeport: Ridiculous! I never wept in my life: our eyes were never given us for that purpose: I own I'm sorry. Though she is a little proud, as I told you, yet she is such a good creature, one can't help being concerned at losing her. If you go, madam, you must write to me; I shall always be glad to do you any service: perhaps we may meet again one day or other, who knows! but be sure you don't forget to write to me.

Miss Lindon: I assure you, sir, I will; and if ever fortune—

Freeport: Fabrice, I'm sure this woman is well-born. I shall expect a letter from you, but don't put too much wit into it.

Fabrice: You will forgive me, madam, but I really don't think you are at liberty to go hence, as Mr. Freeport is bail for you, and must lose five hundred pounds if you leave us.

Miss Lindon: O heaven! another distress! another humiliation! must I then remain here? and my lord—my father too.—

Freeport: [To Fabrice.] O don't let that stop her—there is something in her that charms me—but let her go as soon as she pleases: you don't suppose I value five hundred pounds. Hark'ee, Fabrice, put five hundred more into her portmanteau. I beg, madam, [to Miss Lindon] you will go whenever it is agreeable to you; write to me, and let me see you when you return; for I have really conceived a great esteem and affection for you.

SCENE II.

Lord Murray and Servants at One Part of the Stage, Miss Lindon and the Rest at the Other.

Lord Murray: [To his servants.] Stay you here: and do you run to the court of chancery, and bring me those parchments as soon as they are finished: go you and get things ready at my new house. [Pulls a paper out of his pocket, and reads.] What happiness it will be to make her happy!

Miss Lindon: [To Polly.] O Polly, I am distracted at the sight of him.

Freeport: This lord always comes in unseasonably: he is handsome and well-made, and yet I don't like him: but what's that to me? I have certainly some regard for her; but I am not in love with her.—Madam, your servant.

Miss Lindon: I shall not go, sir, without paying my respects to you.

Freeport: O pray, madam, no ceremony; perhaps it may affect me too much. Don't think I'm in love with you, madam; but I should be glad to see you once more before you go: I shall be in the house, and must see you set out. Go, Fabrice, and help the good gentleman above. I find I have a prodigious regard for this young lady.

SCENE III.

Lord Murray, Miss Lindon

Lord Murray: At length once more I am happy in the sight of all I hold dear on earth. What a house is this for Miss Lindon! but one more worthy of her is prepared: you look down and weep: for heaven's sake what has happened to you? who was that surly looking fellow talking with you? if he is the cause of your uneasiness, he shall soon repent it.

Miss Lindon: Alas! my lord, he is one of the best of men; one who has taken pity on my misfortunes; who has never abandoned, never insulted me; one who never talked to my rival without deigning to look on me; one who, if he had loved me, would not have let three days pass without writing.

Lord Murray: Believe me, when I tell you, I had rather die than merit the least of those cruel reproaches. I absented myself but for your sake, thought of nothing but you, and have served you in spite of yourself: if, on my return here, I found that clamorous revengeful woman, could I help it? I went back again immediately to counteract her fatal designs. My God, not write to you!

Miss Lindon: No.

Lord Murray: I see she has intercepted my letters; her baseness increases, if possible, my passion; may it recall yours! how unkind was it in you to conceal from me your name and condition! a condition so unworthy of you.

Miss Lindon: Who disclosed them to you?

Lord Murray: [Pointing to Polly.] She, your confederate.

Miss Lindon: Did you betray me?

Polly: You betrayed yourself, madam; I served you.

Miss Lindon: You know me then; you know what hatred hath always divided our families: your father was the cause of mine being condemned to death; he reduced me to that wretched state which I endeavored to conceal from you; and you, his son, now dare avow a passion for me!

Lord Murray: I do; I adore you; 'tis what I owe you: my love shall repair the injuries my father did: 'tis the justice of providence: my heart, my fortune, and my life, are at your disposal: let us unite these hostile names. Here is a contract of marriage; shall I hope to see it executed?

Miss Lindon: Alas! my lord, it is impossible; I am going this moment to leave you forever.

Lord Murray: Going? to leave me forever? sooner shall you behold me perish at your feet: am I at last rejected then?

Polly: I say, madam, you must not go; you are always making some desperate resolution: but I shall bring you to yourself again. My lord, you must second me.

Lord Murray: Who could inspire you with this cruel design to fly from me, to render all my cares abortive?

Miss Lindon: My father.

Lord Murray: Your father? where is he? what does he mean to do with you? inform me quickly.

Miss Lindon: He's here, and means to carry me away with him; it is resolved.

Lord Murray: No: by thy dear self I swear, it must not, shall not be: where is he? conduct me to him.

Miss Lindon: My dearest lord, take care; let him not see you: he is come hither to finish his misfortunes by taking away your life, and I have consented to fly with him to divert him from this dreadful resolution.

Lord Murray: Yours is more cruel still; but be assured I fear him not, nay hope one day to make him my friend.—This fellow not returned yet! O heaven! how swift is every evil thing, how slow is every good!

Miss Lindon: My father comes: if you love me, do not let him see you; spare him the horror of such an interview: for heaven's sake retire, at least for a while.

Lord Murray: 'Tis with the utmost regret that I submit; but you command, and I must obey. I will go in, and return with arms that shall make his drop out of his hand.

SCENE IV.

Montross, Miss Lindon.

Montross: Come, my dear daughter, my only comfort and support, let us be gone.

Miss Lindon: O thou unhappy father of a more unhappy daughter, never, never will I leave you; but permit me to stay here a little longer.

Montross: What! after your urgent entreaties that I would go immediately; after having promised to follow me to some desert solitude, where I may forget my disgrace! have you changed your design? have you so soon forgot the tender sentiments you so lately expressed?

Miss Lindon: Indeed, sir, I am not changed: I am incapable of such baseness; I will follow you: but once more let me entreat you, stay a little while: grant but this favor to her who owes to you a life of sorrows; do not refuse me a few precious moments.

Montross: They are indeed precious, and yet you would lavish them away: consider we are every moment in danger of being discovered, that you have yourself been seized, that they are even now in search of me, and that to-morrow you may see your father given up to an ignominious death.

Miss Lindon: Those words are as a clap of thunder to me. I submit, sir: I am ashamed to have stayed so long; but I had a distant hope—no matter; you are my father, and I'll follow you. O me!

SCENE V.

Freeport and Fabrice on One Side of the Stage, Montross and His Daughter on the Other.

Freeport: [To Fabrice.] Her servant has carried the portmanteau back to her chamber: they'll not go yet; I'm glad of that, however. I began to have a sort of liking for her; not that I'm in love with her; but she is so well-bred, there is no parting from her without some uneasiness; a kind of anxiety that I never felt before: there's something very extraordinary in it.

Montross: [To Freeport.] Sir, your servant; we are just going to set out, with hearts full of gratitude to you for past favors: I assure you I never met with a worthier man than yourself: you almost reconcile me to mankind.

Freeport: You are going then, sir, and this lady I suppose: I'm sorry for it: you should have staid a little longer; indeed you should. I have just now thought of something, that, perhaps, might not be disagreeable to you: pray, stay.

SCENE VI.

Lord Murray: [To them, taking a roll of parchment from his servant.] 'Tis well: thank heaven! I have at last got the pledge of my future happiness.

Freeport: [Aside.] A plague on this lord, here he is again: I hate him for being so agreeable.

Montross: [To his daughter, while Lord Murray is talking to his servant.] Who is that man, my dear?

Miss Lindon: It is, sir—it is—O heaven! have mercy on me!

Fabrice: 'Tis my Lord Murray, sir, one of the finest gentlemen in this kingdom, and the most generous.

Montross: Murray! O heaven! my fatal enemy, who comes to insult me, to triumph over my misfortunes [draws his sword] but he shall have my life, or I his.

Miss Lindon: O stop, my father, what would you do?

Montross: Cruel daughter! and is it thus you have betrayed me?

Fabrice: [Stepping between them.] No violence, I beg, sir, in my house; you will ruin me.

Freeport: Why should you hinder people from fighting, if they have a mind to it?

Lord Murray: [At a distance from Montross.] You are the father of that charming woman?

Miss Lindon: O, I die.

Montross: I am, sir; I'll not deny it. Come then, thou cruel son of a still more cruel father, I know thy purpose; come, and take my life.

Fabrice: Again, sir—

Lord Murray: Stop him not: I have that which will disarm him. [Draws his sword.]

Miss Lindon: [Sinking into the arms of Polly.] Cruel man! and dare you—

Lord Murray: Yes, I dare—I am the son of your inveterate foe; and thus [throwing away his sword] I attack you.

Freeport: Here's another for you, sir.

Lord Murray: Now, sir, with one hand strike this guilty breast, and with the other receive this paper—read, and know me.

Montross: What do I see? my pardon signed, my honors restored, my family re-established! O heaven! and is it to you, to Lord Murray, I owe it all. O! my friend, my benefactor, now you triumph more, much more, than if I had fallen by your sword.

Miss Lindon: O unexpected happiness! my lover then is worthy of me.

Lord Murray: O my father, permit me to embrace you.

Montross: How shall I repay such generosity?

Lord Murray: [Pointing to Miss Lindon.] There, sir, is my reward.

Montross: The father and the daughter are both yours forever.

Freeport: [To Fabrice.] My friend, I was afraid this lady was not made for me: however, she is fallen into good hands, and I am satisfied.

End

www.ingramcontent.com/pod-product-compliance
Lightning Source LLC
Chambersburg PA
CBHW031429040426
42444CB00006B/746